AF290310

THE GREAT RECESSION

The burst of the property bubble
and the excesses of speculation

Written by Anastasia Samygin-Cherkaoui
Translated by Rebecca Neal

THE GREAT RECESSION (2007-2009)

THE BURST OF THE PROPERTY BUBBLE AND THE EXCESSES OF SPECULATION

- **When:** 2007-2009.
- **Where:** the crisis began in the USA, before spreading around the world.
- **Context:** when a speculative housing bubble in the USA burst, many homeowners ended up defaulting on their mortgage payments. Subsequently, a high-risk loans mechanism, through which lenders used securitization to transfer their responsibility to other financial organisations, came to light.
- **Key protagonists:**
  - The government-sponsored organisations the Federal National Mortgage Association (FNMA, known colloquially as Fannie Mae) and the Federal Home

Loan Mortgage Corporation (FHLMC, known colloquially as Freddy Mac).
- The major American merchant banks and insurance companies Goldman Sachs, AIG, Lehman Brothers, Morgan Stanley and JPMorgan Chase.
- Michael Burry (American physician and hedge fund manager, born in 1971) and Steve Eisman (American investor, born in 1962), who were among the first investors to foresee the impending subprime mortgage crisis.

- **Key terms:**
  - <u>Securitization</u>: a mechanism introduced in the 1990s which allows banks to sell on the loans they have given out in the form of securities.
  - <u>Subprime loan</u>: a type of loan in the US which involves lending to borrowers who may struggle to pay back the money, in order to purchase property or other goods.

In 2008, the world saw another side to America: when the property bubble burst and the financial crisis hit the country, onlookers learnt of financial practices that left thousands of American households homeless, emptied whole neighbourhoods of their inhabitants, ruined towns and drove numerous banks and insurance companies to bankruptcy.

This year marked the beginning of a localised financial crisis which soon developed into a worldwide economic crisis. Before long, the terms "subprime lending", "toxic assets" and "securitization" began cropping up in everyday conversation and, through investment funds, these toxic assets threatened major European banks. Citizens became aware of the banks' lack of transparency and the fundamental arrogance underlying the expression "too big to fail" used to describe the largest American and European banks. Governments around the world were soon forced to pump billions of dollars into bailout plans to rescue the ailing financial institutions.

As we will see in this guide, 2008 was the year the American dream became a nightmare.

CONTEXT

HARMFUL LENDING MECHANISMS

Subprime loans

Subprime loans were initially introduced in the 1990s to allow a less financially stable section of the population to get on the property ladder, but their purpose changed in the early 2000s, largely because of their higher variable interest rates and the state of the property market, which was booming at that time. The outstanding growth potential of subprime loans, also known as NINJA loans (No income, no job, no assets), attracted the attention of bankers, who planned to sell them on to other financial agents such as banks, insurance companies and investment funds.

But how do these loans work? In return for high, often variable interest rates, subprime mortgages allow households to borrow beyond their means, in the expectation that house prices will continue rising indefinitely. This allows these households to secure credit, sometimes taking out multiple loans for the same property. If borrowers find themselves struggling to make their repayments, they have two options:

- Take out another loan for a higher amount, based on an upwards revision of the value of their property, in order to make the monthly repayments for the initial loan.
- Put their faith in the continued growth of the market and take out a loan to buy an investment property (a property purchased for speculative purposes, which is generally divided into several units to be rented out by the owner or owners). Provided that the property market remains stable, the income from this investment property should theoretically allow them to pay back the initial loan.

Given that these loans have an initial repayment period of two or three years with a fixed, relatively low interest rate before the variable interest rates kick in, borrowers are led to believe that they will be able to pay them back in full. However, in reality borrowers almost always default at the end of the fixed-rate period, forcing them to take out further loans.

Between 2001 and 2007, American mortgage debt almost doubled in absolute terms, while the average mortgage debt per household also increased, from $91 500 to $149 500, with virtually no increase in average household income over the same period (University of North Carolina at Chapel Hill, 2012).

As prices were rising, consumers were saving less and spending and borrowing more. As a result, the total household debt skyrocketed: by 2008, it stood at $14 500 billion, or 134% of household income, compared with $7400 billion at the end of 2000.

Securitization

Through buybacks and interbank lending, the loans granted by a bank were sold on to another, larger bank in the form of securities which could be traded on the markets. The higher the initial borrowing rate, the higher the rate of return on investment would be. As the housing market was assumed to be stable and growing, financial institutions were not wary of mortgages.

High-risk loans were grouped together with

other securities, and consequently ended up in the largest merchant banks as part of "complex" financial products, namely collateralized debt obligations and credit default swaps.

- A **collateralized debt obligation** (CDO) is a mixture of theoretically risky bonds (with a rating of at least B) which, when combined as part of a new financial product, are given a higher rating (AAA) by rating agencies. In the 2015 film *The Big Short*, CDOs are explained using the following metaphor: a cook with fillets of fish that they have not sold (B-rated bonds) but that are not fresh enough to put on the menu as they are decides to make them into a stew, thus creating a new product (CDO) that they can revalue (AAA) and put on the menu for the following days.

BOND CREDIT RATINGS

While shares are parts of capital, bonds are instruments of indebtedness. To give investors an idea of the risk they are running, bonds are given a rating ranging from AAA to D. AAA is used to designate the highest-quality bonds, in terms of both capital and interest payments, while D refers to bonds that are said to be "in default". The intermediate rankings B and C (which are subdivided into BBB, BB, B then CCC, CC and C) apply to increasingly speculative products.

- A **credit default swap** (CDS) is an instrument that was created in the 1990s by Blythe Masters (born in 1969), a managing director at the merchant bank JPMorgan Chase. It is a sort of insurance contract between financial institutions, which can be included in a "pack" of CDOs. Like a conventional insurance contract, it features a buyer and a seller who, in exchange for payment, agrees to cover the risk of default on the debt payments. If the risk does not come to pass, the insurer collects their payment and increases their assets without investing anything in return. However, if the risk does come to pass, they will have to pay out sums which could be considerable. In this case, unlike with traditional insurance contracts, the seller is under no obligation to maintain a reserve, meaning that they may have to cover risks beyond their means. Furthermore, as these payments are uncertain, they are not recorded on the balance sheets. This means that, while assets appear when the payments are made, the risks are somewhat "hidden". Consequently, a CDS encourages both buyers and sellers to take greater risks.

The consequence (and the aim) of securitization is therefore to transfer the risk associated with a loan from the operator that granted it to one or more distinct financial operators. This marked a profound shift in the role of the banker: whereas previously, banks were responsible if their clients defaulted on their payments and had to guard against this risk for the entire duration of their contracts, they could now cast off this risk, and therefore their responsibility.

This approach diminished the importance of risk analysis, which became almost negligible. Furthermore, these products ultimately became so complex that it was impossible to tell which institutions held what. In the end, this system of dilution proved ineffective, and the securities containing high-risk loans ended up concentrated within large banks and insurance companies.

As we can clearly see, this mechanism was harmful, and it became so widespread that before long the products comprising subprime loans became a ticking timebomb for banks. In 1998, subprime loans represented around 2.8% of American mortgages (Bartnik, 2015), but by the end of 2006 this figure had risen to over 20% (Karabell, 2014). By 2007, 40% of the new mortgages granted were subprime mortgages.

SPECULATION AND LEVERAGE

When we consider the additional fact that 40% of these subprime loans were speculative, in that they were taken out on investment properties or second homes (University of North Carolina at Chapel Hill, 2012), we can see that these loans carried significant risks. When the market collapsed, prices in this speculative sector dropped far faster than those in the residential market.

The danger associated with the securitization of high-risk loans was exacerbated by what is known as leverage, meaning the use of borrowed funds to purchase assets. Leverage is calculated based on the relationship between financial return and economic return.

The main difference between these two ostensibly similar concepts lies in their denominator: while financial return is calculated in relation to equity, meaning the borrower's real contribution, economic return is calculated based on all the capital involved, including loans. When the profit obtained thanks to loans is higher than the value of the debt, the leverage is positive and the value of the borrower's equity increases. Shareholders consequently receive high dividends, which are especially attractive given that:

- they only contribute part of the value of the investment;
- the borrowing rate is low;
- profits are high.

Good to know

"Leverage" refers to positive rates, whereas negative rates are referred to using the term "boomerang effect".

Case study

Take the example of the purchase of an investment property with a private contribution of 20%. The leverage ratio will be 4 (80% loan/20% own funds). The final result will be positive if the rent received is higher than the cost of credit and if the estimated value of the property increases.

- Purchase of the property: £200 000.
- Own contribution: £40 000.
- Loan: £160 000.
- Borrowing rate: 2%.
- Annual income from rent: £7200 (£600 per month).

The annual financial return can therefore be calculated by subtracting taxes (£0, as income from rent is tax-free) and the cost of credit (£3200) from the rent received (£7200), giving a total of £4000. Comparing this total with the amount of own capital gives 10% (£4000/£40 000). Economic return can be calculated by dividing the £7200 of rent received by the total amount of capital used to purchase the property (£200 000), giving 3.6%.

The leverage ratio is 4, and is calculated by dividing debt (£160 000) by own funds (£40 000). A simplified way of calculating leverage is to work out the difference between the rate of economic return (3.6%) and the rate of interest on the loan (in this case, 2%). When this rate is positive, the leverage is also positive, and if all goes well it will increase over time with:

- rent indexation;
- the increased value of the property;
- the progressive reduction of the proportion of interest in the repayment of the loan.

If the loan is a subprime loan, meaning that no initial capital is contributed, the leverage ratio is high but the leverage will be zero or negative (if the property is overvalued and/or the borrower is immediately able to borrow a greater amount than its estimated value). Even with the income from rent, the financial return will be negative from the start, given that little or no own funds will be contributed, which in turn means that interest rates will be higher.

- Purchase of the property: £200 000.
- Loan: 110% of the value of the property, mea-

ning £220 000 at 4% interest, giving a cost of credit of £8800.

- Annual income from rent: £7200 (£600 per month).

In this case, the economic return is 3.3%, or £7200 (rent received) over £220 000 (capital employed). The problem is that this is lower than the interest rate (4%). We therefore obtain a negative leverage of 0.7%.

Now, imagine that a person wants to buy a new property for £180 000 (which will also be the value of their loan), and that to do so they use their first property (valued at £200 000) as a guarantee. Suppose that the income from rent for this new property is also £7200. According to these criteria, the leverage is 1.1% (£200 000 own contribution and £180 000 loan). The economic profitability will be £7200 (income from rent) over the £380 000 total contribution (own funds plus debt), giving us 1.9%.

However, if the income from rent is £6000 rather than £7200, the economic return drops to 1.57%. If the borrowing rate is 2%, the leverage will once again be negative. This example provides a clear illustration of the dangerous domino effect that this practice can lead to.

The banks' indifference

It is banks' job to lend more than they actually possess, which inevitably entails risks in cases of non-payment. The more clients are unable to re-pay their debts, the greater this risk will be. This means that safeguards are vital in order to limit leverage and keep risky speculative activities separate from traditional activities. To this end, it is often recommended that deposit banks be kept separate from merchant banks and investment banks.

Investment funds engage in purely speculative activity, which is why they can offer high interest rates. At the same time, the level of risk associated with their activities is high, which means that they can also tolerate high leverage. That said, when they went bust, the American bank Bear Stearns and the investment fund Carlyle Capital Group had leverage ratios of 35 and 32 respectively, whereas most economics textbooks suggest that the leverage ratio should remain between 2 and 5 (Lordon, 2008).

To go back to our previous example, if the individual contributes £40 000 of their own funds, a leverage ratio of 30 means that they risk taking on £1.2 million of debt (as the leverage ratio corresponds to the relationship between debt and own funds).

HOW THE CRISIS PLAYED OUT

By 2007, all the ingredients for a crisis were in place:

- interest rates increased as the period of attractive low fixed rates came to an end and variable rates came into effect;
- a significant number of households were unable to repay their loans;
- the non-payment rate reached 15%.

A total of eight million households lost their homes that year, including both tenants whose landlords were affected by the crisis and homeowners. Before long there were a million foreclosures per year, and this rate showed no signs of diminishing in subsequent years. In September 2011, the Federal Reserve estimated that the rate of forced sales still stood at 40%. A report by the French treasury service in 2009 estimated that there would be a total of 17 million property foreclosures between the start of the crisis in 2006 and the return to normality expected in 2015 (Sorbe, 2009).

Banks suddenly realised the seriousness of the threat posed by toxic assets, meaning the presence of high-risk speculative assets that were not identified as such, in their accounts. As speculative activities were inextricably linked to "traditional" activities, they both collapsed at the same time. This can be seen in the play *D'un retournement l'autre. Comédie sérieuse sur la crise financière* ("From one turn to another: serious comedy on the financial crisis") by the French economist and sociologist Frédéric Lordon (born in 1962), which compares the toxic assets to waste which leaves the banks only to find a way back in, submerging bankers under the deluge.

In 2009, an estimated 23% of homeowners who were yet to repay their mortgages had lower total assets than the sum borrowed. However, this average figure of 23% conceals significant regional variations: in Nevada, this problem of property overvaluation affected 65% of homeowners, while the figure stood at 48% in Arizona and 45% in Florida (Halimi, 2010). Moreover, in 2012, Florida was the state with the highest percentage of borrowers who were unable to pay back their loans, at 45% (University of North Carolina at Chapel Hill, 2012).

FROM THE SUBPRIME MORTGAGE CRISIS TO THE BANKING AND FINANCIAL CRISIS

On 10 July 2007, the rating agency Moody's downgraded the rating of 400 securities linked to subprime loans, and the following week the investment bank Bear Stearns revealed that its investment fund had lost half its value due to subprime loans.

At the start of August 2007, other financial establishments, which were located both within the USA and as far afield as Europe and Australia, indicated that they had been affected by the beginning of the crisis as a result of securitization. In France, BNP Paribas suspended three investment funds with connections to subprime loans. Later that month, central banks began injecting funds into ailing financial institutions in order to keep them afloat. For example, the Bank of America came to the assistance of Countrywide

Financial, the first American mortgage lender at risk of bankruptcy, with a $2 billion capital injection. This substantial aid nonetheless proved insufficient, and was followed by further capital injections in September of the same year.

On 14 September 2007, the Bank of England announced that it had been forced to grant an emergency loan to Northern Rock, the fifth-largest mortgage-lending institution in the country. The crisis was beginning to spread, but it was still far from its height, which was reached the following year.

In December 2007, countries' central banks administered further cash injections, which led to a rebound on the stock markets and rising interest rates in America. To a certain extent, this increase worsened the subprime mortgage crisis, as least for loans with variable interest rates which were linked to the interest rates of the Federal Reserve.

In March 2008, the Federal Reserve provided a further injection of liquidity by granting a $30 billion loan to the bank JPMorgan Chase.

On 30 July of that year, the American president George W. Bush (born in 1946) took a series of measures, including the creation of a $300 billion fund to help struggling mortgage borrowers and the provision of emergency aid to the government-sponsored organisations Freddie Mac and Fannie Mae. In spite of these efforts, the US government took control of both organisations, at an estimated potential cost of $200 billion.

FROM THE BANKING AND FINANCIAL CRISIS TO THE WORLDWIDE ECONOMIC CRISIS

On 15, 16 and 18 September, the situation swiftly deteriorated further:

- on 15 September, the investment bank Lehman Brothers declared bankruptcy;
- on 16 September, the Federal Reserve granted a $85 billion loan to the insurer AIG, which stood on the brink of bankruptcy;
- on 18 September, the Federal Reserve was forced to inject $180 billion into the struggling markets, while the European Central Bank (ECB) did the same to the tune of $40 billion.

At the end of the month, Belgium, the Netherlands, Luxembourg and France rushed to the assistance of BNP Paribas (with partial nationalisation, since the state has more resources at its disposal than a private company and is less likely to go bankrupt) and Dexia (with an equity takeout of €6.4 billion).

The following month, the Emergency Economic Stabilization Act of 2008, a bailout plan for American banks, set aside at least $700 billion of public funds to buy back risky loans and stabilise the markets. In Europe, the G7 countries agreed to launch a similar rescue plan for the European financial system. A few days later, on 13 October, the French government decided to inject €10.5 billion into the six largest banks in the country.

In April 2008, the International Monetary Fund (IMF) estimated the total cost of the crisis at $1000 billion, while the Organisation for Economic Cooperation and Development (OECD) put the losses linked to subprime loans at $422 billion.

As we can see, the sums involved were staggering. The size of the crisis – banks lost an estimated total of $700 billion (Couderc and Montel-Dumont, 2010) – as well as its scope and consequences make it a key event in contemporary economic history.

IMPACT

GOVERNMENT BAILOUTS

Although the initial aim in the USA was for private organisations to reach agreements among themselves, the government was still forced to intervene: it spent $29 billion to bail out Bear Steans and a further $200 billion to Freddie Mac and Fannie Mae. It also helped to rescue the insurer AIG – whose potential bankruptcy was expected to be catastrophic – through an injection of $85 billion for a 79.9% equity stake.

Conversely, the state did not intervene to help Lehman Brothers, and its collapse had major repercussions in Europe, notably due to its many subsidiaries on the continent. For example, the two largest banks in France each sustained estimated losses of €500 million. The toxic assets held in European banks therefore came to light as a direct result of the collapse of Lehman Brothers.

At the same time, the UK government was forced

to grant loans of approximately £25 billion and guarantees of approximately £30 billion to save Northern Rock.

Germany provided funding though public and private consortiums: it bailed out regional public banks with €8 billion provided by a larger public body, as well as a €26 billion loan granted by a public/private consortium to rescue the bank Hypo Real Estate.

The cases of Fortis and Dexia are more complex. As the €16.8 billion provided jointly by Belgium and the Netherlands proved insufficient to rescue Fortis, the two states decided to nationalise parts of the Belgian-Dutch financial company:

- Firstly, the Netherlands nationalised Fortis NL and granted an additional €34 billion in credit.
- Belgium nationalised Fortis Bank Belgium and Fortis Assurance. These two divisions were subsequently taken over by the French bank BNP Paribas, which acquired a 100% stake in Fortis Assurance and a 75% stake in Fortis Bank Belgium. Belgium retained a share of just over 11% in BNP Paribas, and still held 90% of the risky assets of the defunct Fortis

Bank Belgium, which were isolated in a bad bank so that they could be resold at the best possible price. The purpose of bad banks is to clean up banks' balance sheets by removing bad assets so that they can avoid bankruptcy. It is worth noting that not all the risky assets isolated in this way will pose problems, so later on they may be redeemed or renegotiated. Furthermore, it is important to win back the confidence of "traditional" customers and investors, which means clearly identifying any risky investments among their assets.

The three countries involved with Dexia (Belgium, France and Luxembourg) organised a joint rescue plan. Together, they provided a capital injection of €6.4 billion and a guarantee covering 100% of Dexia's new liabilities towards other bodies.

THE BANKS PAY UP

In the USA, five major banks (Wells Fargo, Bank of America, JPMorgan Chase, Citibank and Ally Financial) concluded an agreement worth a total of $25 billion to prevent legal proceedings over improper foreclosures. In addition to this collective fine, several of the banks also paid individual fines:

- JPMorgan Chase agreed to pay $13 billion as part of a private arrangement to compensate affected individuals.
- The Bank of America paid $11.6 billion to the refinancing organisation Fannie Mae, and in June 2011 paid out $8.5 billion in compensation to a group of investors. Finally, at the start of 2014, the bank was found guilty of defrauding Fannie Mae and Freddie Mac by deliberately concealing the risky nature of some of its assets, and was forced to pay a further fine of $9.5 billion.
- Citigroup was hit with a $7 billion fine for selling securities linked to subprime loans.

CONCERNS OVER SOVEREIGN DEBT

As we have seen, the heavy blow to banks' liquidity due to the plummeting value of their assets was the first major consequence of the crisis, and before long many of them had to be bailed out with public money.

This also led to increased wariness regarding bad assets, and many customers no longer trusted their banks. Amid mounting uncertainty, the conditions that private individuals and businesses had to meet to access credit became more stringent.

While spending increases during periods of growth, it decreases during periods of recession. During the Great Recession, this worsened the situation: in addition to bankruptcies, many jobs were lost, not renewed (fixed-term contracts, interim contracts, failure to replace departing employees) or simply not created. Public finances were depleted as a result of bailout plans for banks and the burgeoning recession, at a time when public debt was already high.

This left national governments facing a dilemma:

• they could implement economic recovery programmes, which would have a negative impact on public finances in the short term;
• alternatively, they could limit public spending through austerity measures, which risked worsening the recession.

The governments of certain countries, including Greece, Spain and Portugal, deemed the risk of default to be critical. To illustrate the magnitude of the threat, 80% of Greece's national debt was held in foreign banks. This meant that the crisis now affected countries' sovereign debt.

Sovereign debt had traditionally been viewed as risk-free, but this blind faith was now being shaken: if the situation was such that part of the national debt would never be repaid, the apparently unshakeable solvency of states would crumble. In case of bankruptcy, creditors would be forced to write off these debts. But could a country within the European economic and monetary union really go bankrupt?

Like any customers with limited creditworthiness, countries deemed to be high-risk faced higher borrowing rates. For example, in 2010 Greece was forced to take out loans with an interest rate of over 9%, compared with around 5% in 2008 and 2009. This situation only got worse in the years that followed: the interest rate subsequently rose even further, to 15.75% in 2011 and 22.5% in 2012. For comparison, the long-term bond rates (ten years) were 2.74% in 2010, 2.61% in 2011 and 1.5% in 2012 for Germany, and 3.46% in 2010, 4.23% in 2011 and 3% in 2012 for Belgium. Similarly, in 2015 the borrowing rates for Germany and Belgium dipped below 1%, but the corresponding rates for Greece were still almost 10%.

REFLECTIONS ON ECONOMIC EQUITY

Interactions between governments and banks are complex. Part of the state's role is to control and regulate the financial sector (although, as we have seen, they have largely fallen short in this responsibility), but at the same time they need the banks in order to secure loans. As such, the state's role is complex: it is at once a customer of the banks and the authority responsible for their oversight. As banks grow stronger, the state's power over them becomes more limited. Indeed, the majority of government bonds are purchased by national, European and international banks.

The initial acquiring bank can subsequently resell this debt after a certain period of time. It can then be negotiated on the market and becomes available to other investors. To illustrate this point, in 2010 Agence France Trésor (the organisation tasked with managing the state's debts and cash requirements) estimated that one third of the French national debt was held by French investors, another third was held by other European investors, and the final third by foreign investors from outside Europe.

Around 15 years ago, the proportion of the national debt held by investors from outside Europe was significantly lower, at 20% (Pottier, 2011). Problems may arise if these foreign investors have different concerns (from an environment or ethical point of view, for example) from the states whose debt they hold. This in turn reduces states' freedom of action.

If a country's debt is held by a handful of investors, the country will effectively be at their mercy. For example, in the mid-1980s, Pablo Escobar (Colombian drug lord, 1949-1993) offered to buy Colombia's national debt in exchange for a passage into politics.

In the wake of the 2008 crisis, initiatives related to ethical, local, sustainable and responsible finance emerged, but their impact within the financial sector as a whole remains minor.

Furthermore, a closer look at these initiatives reveals that there is nothing new about them: they were already an integral part of the "old" banks (meaning public banks and banks prior to the intervention of consortiums), such as Crédit communal in Belgium and Crédit municipal in France.

Finance as part of a liberal capitalist economy does not necessarily comprise an ethical dimension, but its socio-economic consequences have an undeniable impact on the fate of society of a whole. Given that the world is undergoing a process of widespread financialization, the issues raised by the financial sector are more pertinent than ever.

In this context, we are led to ask whether the financial sector can continue to privatise profits while pooling risks in the case of failure. Similarly, it is hard to justify the way the sector meddles in the real economy and uses money to make money, then leaves taxpayers to clean up the mess when its activities spiral out of control.

The aim of finance should be to see money not as a means to an end, but as an end in itself, and it is high time for this shift in perspective to take place.

THE SITUATION TODAY

What have we learnt from the excesses of 2008? Are loans today any safer than they were back then? Sadly, this does not seem to be the case. Subprime loans are making a comeback, especially for consumer lending. In the USA, new loans are being granted to high-risk borrowers, this time to buy cars, while the non-payment rates for these loans have reached record levels.

Furthermore, the state of student loans in the USA is becoming worrying (Lauer, 2015), and the Federal Reserve estimates that they total $1160 billion, equivalent to an average of around $30 000 per borrower.

What will happen if these borrowers do not find employment? In June 2014, President Obama (born in 1961) acknowledged the problem and decided to introduce a repayment cap of 10% of the graduate's salary. This limit was already in place for loans taken out after 2007; Obama's measure broadened access to borrowers who took out loans before that date. In spite of this progress, the financial sector as a whole still seems largely indifferent to the real people behind the figures.

SUMMARY

- The financial crisis in 2008 was triggered by the burst of the speculative property bubble in the USA.
- This property speculation was followed by economic speculation, which was made possible by the mechanisms of securitization and complex financial products known as collateralized debt obligations and credit default swaps.
- These products allowed lenders not only to avoid the risk linked to credit, but also to insure, reinsure and speculate on the same initial value. In this way, bad assets were turned into exchangeable assets whose value could be increased.
- This is why the crisis reached such colossal proportions, with the total value of subprime mortgages estimated at $1100 billion. Speculation and leverage were responsible for the scale and repercussions of the crisis.
- The crisis also revealed the interconnectedness of banks and securitization on an international

scale. In the end, it was impossible to tell who held what, which meant that potentially toxic assets were not only not clearly identified as such, but were also dispersed throughout a large number of financial institutions.

- Between 2007 and 2014, the worldwide public debt ratio experienced average growth of between 5.8% (before the crisis) and 9.7%. In concrete terms, this represents an additional $25 000 billion of public debt.

We want to hear from you!
Leave a comment on your online library
and share your favourite books on social media!

FURTHER READING

BIBLIOGRAPHY

- Bartnik, M. (2015) Comprendre la crise des subprimes en quatre questions simples. *Le Figaro*. [Online]. [Accessed 18 December 2017]. Available from: <http://www.lefigaro.fr/economie/le-scan-eco/explicateur/2015/09/03/29004-20150903ARTFIG00126-la-crise-des-subprimes-en-quatre-questions.php>

- Bernard, P. (2012) A Orlando, les expulsés du "rêve américain" vivent un enfer. *Le Monde*. [Online]. [Accessed 18 December 2017]. Available from: <http://www.lemonde.fr/ameriques/article/2012/04/23/a-orlando-les-expulses-du-reve-americain-vivent-un-enfer_1689699_3222.html>

- Couderc, N. and Montel-Dumont, O. (2010) D'une crise à l'autre. Des subprimes à la crise mondiale. *Les politiques économiques à l'épreuve de la crise.* Cahiers français n° 595.

- (2008) Crise financière 2007-2008 : les raisons du désordre mondial – chronologie. *La documentation française.* [Online]. [Accessed 18 December 2017]. Available from: <http://www.stat.unc.edu/faculty/cji/fys/2012/Subprime%20mortgage%20

crisis.pdf>

- Delion, A. (2008) La crise financière et le retour des États. *Revue française d'administration*. 128, pp. 799-816.

- Halimi, S. (2010) « Cleveland contre Wall Street », les subprime au cinéma. *Le Monde Diplomatique*. [Online]. [Accessed 18 December 2017]. Available from: <https://www.monde-diplomatique.fr/carnet/2010-08-20-Cleveland-contre-Wall-Street>

- Karabell, Z. (2014) Subprime Loans Are Back! *Slate*. [Online]. [Accessed 18 December 2017]. Available from: <http://www.slate.com/articles/business/moneybox/2014/09/the_return_of_the_subprime_loan_believe_it_or_not_it_s_a_good_thing.html>

- Lauer, S. (2015) Les dettes des étudiants inquiètent les Etats-Unis. *Le Monde*. [Online]. [Accessed 18 December 2017]. Available from: <http://www.lemonde.fr/economie/article/2015/02/18/les-dettes-des-etudiants-inquietent-les-etats-unis_4578459_3234.html>

- (2014) Les Etats-Unis, spécialiste des amendes records pour les banques. *Le Monde*. [Online]. [Accessed 18 December 2017]. Available from: <http://www.lemonde.fr/economie/article/2014/07/14/les-dix-plus-grosses-amendes-infligees-par-les-etats-unis-aux-banques-en-trois-ans_4456986_3234.html>

- Lordon, F. (2011) *D'un retournement l'autre*. Paris: Seuil.

- Lordon, F. (2008) Quatre principes et neuf pro-
positions pour en finir avec les crises financières.
Le Monde Diplomatique. [Online]. [Accessed
18 December 2017]. Available from: <https://blog.
mondediplo.net/2008-04-23-Quatre-principes-et-
neuf-propositions-pour-en>

- Pottier, J-M. (2011) Comment on achète de la dette
publique. *Slate.fr.* [Online]. [Accessed 18 December
2017]. Available from: <http://www.slate.fr/
story/32511/dette-France-marches>

- Sorbe, S. (2009) Saisies immobilières aux
États-Unis et pertes des institutions financières.
Trésor-Eco. 9.

- (2012) Subprime Mortgage Crisis. *University of
North Carolina at Chapel Hill, Department of
Statistics and Operations Research.* [Online].
[Accessed 18 December 2017]. Available from:
<http://www.ladocumentationfrancaise.fr/
dossiers/crise-financiere-2007-2008/chronologie.
shtml>

- (2017) Long-term interest rates. *OECD Data.*
[Online]. [Accessed 18 December 2017]. Available
from: <https://data.oecd.org/interest/long-term-
interest-rates.htm>

ADDITIONAL SOURCES

- Lewis, M (2011) *The Big Short: Inside the Doomsday Machine*. London: Penguin.

- Sandel, M. (2013) *What Money Can't Buy: The Moral Limits of Markets*. London: Penguin.

FILMS

- *Margin Call*. (2011) [Film]. J.C. Chandor. Dir. USA: Before the Door Pictures.

- *The Big Short*. (2015) [Film]. Adam McKay. Dir. USA: Plan B Entertainment, Regency Enterprises.

50MINUTES.com

IMPROVE YOUR GENERAL KNOWLEDGE

IN A BLINK OF AN EYE !

www.50minutes.com

www.50minutes.com

Ebook EAN: 9782808007030

Paperback EAN: 9782808007740

Legal Deposit: D/2017/12603/966

Cover: © Primento

Digital conception by Primento, the digital partner of publishers.